LESS

IS

MORE

WHAT PEOPLE ARE SAYING ABOUT *LESS IS MORE*

In a world that holds stubbornly to the belief that more is more, this gift of a book invites us to discover that in fact less is more, and crucially, how to live into and in that liberating truth. We have been privileged to be part of Lou's personal journey, watching her become more as she simplified her life and made room for God to bring healing and wholeness. Lou combines honesty and vulnerability as she shares her own story with profound insights from scripture and practical encouragement on how to embrace a life of less in order to find the more that only God can give. We wholeheartedly commend this book to anyone looking to embrace life in all its fullness, seeking to discover meaning and purpose in their lives and to find liberation from past pain and all that hinders them.

RICH & KATH JOHNSON, VICAR OF ALL SAINTS WORCESTER AND NEW WINE NATIONAL LEADERSHIP TEAM

Lou's vulnerability is a gift to her readers; giving us permission to be honest with ourselves and others. Her writing helps us to articulate truths in our souls which had perhaps gone unrealised, encouraging us to move into a new season of freedom.

SUSANNA WRIGHT, WRITER AND FILM PRODUCER, NOSCO FILMS

I read this in one sitting with tears rolling down my face. Beautifully written; powerfully honest. This book moved me deeply and filled me with hope in a God who is there and who cares.

SIMON PONSONBY, BIBLE TEACHER AND AUTHOR, ST ALDATES CHURCH

LESS

IS

MORE

LOU SHOREY

Copyright © 2019 Lou Shorey

All rights reserved.

Kids, may you always know that your less is enough.

Beloved,

As you open the pages of this book, I pray you will know how loved and wanted you are and the catalyst for good that lies within your soul. You are a gift from God to the world. Your presence is needed wherever you find yourself: in the office or at the kitchen table; at the school gate or on the train; in the gym or on the dog walk or running errands on the high street. You are a vessel of God's glory and He is ready and waiting to use you – if you are willing. The trouble is that society and church, at times, make us believe that who we are is not enough. It is time to shake this off and step into the fullness of life that Jesus intends for us.

You may recognise it as a line from a poem, a fashionista's quip or an architect's infamous quote, "less is more." Yet better still it is the tender whisper of God's heart to those devoid of purpose and meaning.

Less is More aims to rouse you from your hiding, uncover your shame and challenge the temptation to look the part. It reminds us all to stop promoting platforms and the pursuit of perfectionism and instead to become people who create safe places for others to be vulnerable and usher in God's goodness. It encourages us to process our pain, whilst holding gently to the truth of who we really are. It points to Jesus, the King of Kings, the One who is more than we could ever need yet who the world tells us is not enough. Its petition is to live courageously and triumphantly in spite of our shortcomings and to acknowledge our condition, whilst knowing that *our failures are God's opportunity to do something glorious.*

Less is More is an invitation to an abundant life with Jesus. Contained within these pages is not a justification for a 'prosperity gospel', but *the* gospel – the glorious, good news that God is the God of the multitude and the maximum. It is an invitation to those who wrestle with doubt, fear and a sense of feeling 'less than'. It reminds us that our brokenness doesn't need to stop us living loved but with Jesus we can continue with forward momentum to something deeper, wider, higher and more.

My prayer is that as you read these pages, your feelings of inferiority and worthlessness are drowned out by the whisper of love from our God of more!

Lou x

So, keep your thoughts continually fixed on all that is authentic and real, honourable and admirable, beautiful and respectful, pure and holy, merciful and kind. And fasten your thoughts on every glorious work of God, praising Him always.

PHILIPPIANS 4:8-10

The Passion Translation

One
MIND-LESS
01

Two
FATHER-LESS
15

Three
TRUTH-LESS
31

Four
GOD-LESS
43

Five
PURPOSE-LESS
55

One
MIND-LESS

After giving birth to my daughter, I was presenting a bit more than the 'baby blues'. I was stressed and angry, shouting all the time and I was lacking peace. I was drinking every night to numb the pain and relieve the stress; speeding down a helter-skelter of despair, not sure when the end would be in sight, or if I would ever land safely. When I eventually saw the GP, it was because I wasn't sure what a normal level of stress was anymore. Of course, we all have stress in life, but I'd lost the plot. At my best, I was singing in church, with tears streaming down my face. At my worst, after having our third child, I went to bed with a handful of paracetamol tablets: too scared to live, but too scared to die.

I was full to the brim with pain. I was depressed and anxious, which in my case was largely down to symptoms of perfectionism, control and fear. I was trying to control everyone and everything around me.

I wanted my life to be perfect. I would get angry because the kids wouldn't do what I asked, and I was frustrated when things didn't go the way that I had planned. I sought to control my environment and yet instead of finding peace, I became increasingly riddled with fear. Fear that I would always be like this. Fear that people would know I couldn't cope. Fear that people would see that I didn't have it all together. Fear that I wasn't good enough in anyone's sight, least of all God's. Fear that my brokenness would slam doors in my face rather than open them. Fear that I was unqualified, incapable and not good enough.

FEAR THAT MY IMPERFECTION MADE ME ETERNALLY FLAWED AND PERMANENTLY USELESS.

Fear that one day I would burst into an ocean of tears, of which there would be no end. I lived daily, with a suffocating fear that my crippling feeling of worthlessness could never and would never be fully overcome by God's gift of more.

So, at the GP surgery it all reached a head and I was diagnosed with severe depression. How I was living clearly wasn't working but I was unable to work out how to resolve it. I realise now that I was living under a black cloud of depression, self-loathing and condemnation. My state is so eloquently described here in Romans 8:1-2 in The Message: "With the arrival of Jesus, the Messiah, that fateful dilemma (the battle of being torn one way or another) is resolved. Those who enter into Christ's being-here-for-us no longer have to live under a continuous, low-lying black cloud."

Not living in freedom is depressing; depression is a "low-lying black cloud" that brilliantly sets the stage for the power of 'less' to take hold: self-condemnation, doubt, fear, suicide - you name it, one or more of these thoughts will be cast. Depression is a curse that needs to be broken. It is robbing generations of godly thinking and courageous living.

I knew that I needed to find my way through. I needed help, which I gladly received in pill and counselling form and I needed more of Jesus. I needed Him to come through for me. I needed Him to prove Himself, to deliver, to do what He said He could do. I needed the power of the cross again and again and again. I needed more of Him to set me free and to counter my sense of loss with more of His love, purpose and presence. More than this, I needed to start being honest about my struggle, my pain and my brokenness. I needed to stop being afraid – scared of my story and fearful about telling it. Brené Brown writes in *The Gifts of Imperfection*, that "owning our story and loving ourselves through the process is the bravest thing that we will ever do [yet] the irony is that we attempt to disown our difficult stories to appear more whole or more acceptable."

We all have struggles; we all have pain. We live in a culture of 'fake it to make it', both in and out of church. We've got to stop leaving our real selves outside the church and come as we are. We have to turn the tide on the long-held tradition that vulnerability is weakness and believe that telling our story is a gateway to real and life-giving relationship.

BEING HONEST ABOUT OUR IMPERFECTIONS AND SHORTCOMINGS IS FOOD FOR SOMEONE ELSE'S SOUL.

I had fallen into the enemy's trap – I had been convinced that nothing I could say or do could make me useful to God and His mission. I thought looking holy and whole was the goal. I thought if I kept my mouth shut and my tears from pouring, then people would think I was doing okay and borderline perfect. I was surrounded by smoke and mirrors. The trouble is the smoke fades, the mirrors break and all you are left with is a pile of shattered glass and a broken heart.

Simon P Walker, in *The Undefended Leader*, writes about 'Impression Management'. He describes it as "the selective revealing or concealing of our personal story in order to secure the response we need from our audience." Walker goes on to say, "when we make ourselves vulnerable, we risk rejection and judgement."

We conceal ourselves because we fear that being real will push others away. Yet being exactly who we are, as Christ intended, warts and all, is the perfect remedy to build community and to change the world.

Our vulnerability is a door opener, our brokenness is the gateway to a life of more. Our failings are precisely what we need to keep us humble, reliant on God and best of all, full of story after story of what God has done to transform us and it is this story, *your* story that your neighbours and your work colleagues need to urgently hear.

If we are not honest about our pain – whether we are angry or depressed – and if we don't welcome God in with His gift of 'more', we become isolated and limited and this is precisely how the enemy unleashes his power in our lives. If we listen to the whispers of the enemy – "you're not good enough, you're useless, you're not handsome enough, you're not holy enough" - we become cut off from God, unintentionally limiting the power of His work, simply because we lose perspective. Any courage we had left is trampled all over.

We have to fight back. We have to take back the ground which is God's and which is fertile for truth that changes us. Scripture reminds that, "we can demolish every deceptive fantasy that opposes God and break through every arrogant attitude that is raised up in defiance of the true knowledge of God. We capture, like prisoners of war, every thought and insist that it bow in obedience to the Anointed One" (2 Corinthians 10:15, The Passion Translation). We need to access the tools that God has given us through His word and prayer. By putting on the armour of God each day we will get stronger. This is the promise of God!

Again, we read in Scripture: "God is strong, and He wants you strong. So, take everything the Master has set out for you, well-made weapons of the best materials. And put them to use so you will be able to stand up to everything the Devil throws your way. This is no afternoon athletic contest that we'll walk away from and forget about in a couple of hours. This is for keeps, a life-or-death fight to the finish against the

Devil and all his angels. Be prepared. You're up against far more than you can handle on your own. Take all the help you can get, every weapon God has issued, so that when it's all over but the shouting you'll still be on your feet. Truth, righteousness, peace, faith, and salvation are more than words. Learn how to apply them. You'll need them throughout your life. God's Word is an indispensable weapon. In the same way, prayer is essential in this ongoing warfare. Pray hard and long. Pray for your brothers and sisters. Keep your eyes open. Keep each other's spirits up so that no one falls behind or drops out" (Ephesians 6:10-18, The Message).

We need to put on the armour of God and step into battle. We need to be ready to engage with the challenge and be prepared, with God, to take territory that has been ruled by the enemy for far too long. We need to start choosing to believe His promises and enlarge our thinking, our self-belief and our belief in Him. The catalyst for change starts in the mind.

The battle for the mind is real. I know, I've

experienced it. It's painful and it's cruel but it is a battle that can be won. We need to move from being slave to our thinking to allowing God to be Lord of it. We are to be transformed by the renewal of our mind (Romans 12:2). So it follows that when we have a greater sense of whose we are and are able to focus on what is good, true, pure and noble, we start to notice our words change and grow in confidence in telling others who we are and where we've come from. One of our church leaders shared a story as he preached recently, talking about an addiction he had struggled with and is now free from. As he shared, I wept. I wept for him and his courage. I hope that because he shared his story, others would have been encouraged to do the same.

OUR VULNERABILITY IS THE MOST BEAUTIFUL GIFT WE CAN GIVE EACH OTHER.

Vulnerability connects us and it strengthens us. It is the key to unlocking our sense of wholeness, the truth about ourselves and our courage as Brown describes. I want that life and that connectedness, yet do I want to be vulnerable? No, not especially, but if I really want to embrace a greater freedom in my life, then I guess I would be foolish not to.

Feeling less than perfect is the worst feeling in the world. Feeling like you've failed is soul destroying. Feeling like you are not enough is depressing. I am one of those people who has been prone to confusing the pursuit of wholeness with a merciless attainment of perfectionism at all costs. The good news is that perfectionism is not the goal. The call of God on our lives is. The attainment of this goal is not down to us, solely. It is received by Him and it is He that is at work within us.

Paul's famous vow to "press on towards the goal for the prize of the upward call of God in Christ Jesus" (Philippians 3:14) is motivating indeed, as we are challenged to think about changing our mindset, our perspective and focus. Paul had a sense of something higher, something else that allowed him to move through his despair and affliction. He was able to fully embrace and surrender to the power of God at work, through his brokenness. Likewise, it is only in acknowledging the truth of our condition that we can be fully alive and it's only in having courage not to "look back" as Paul writes, that we will be fully restored.

OUR FAILURES ARE GOD'S OPPORTUNITY TO DO SOMETHING GLORIOUS.

What a revelation that is for us. How wonderful to know that our pain and our sense of 'less' is not the end of the story.

As one commentator notes, Paul's focus is on forward momentum, not prior mistakes and so here is our challenge: we are to focus on Jesus to move forward. When we are tempted to look back and lament our past mistakes and failings, we are to turn again to Jesus, look full into His face and trust Him. This is the good news that we can move through these difficult times and that we can have hope.

We don't have to be 'mindless' as the title of this

chapter suggests. We don't have to remain caught in a web of depression and anxiety, or low-self-esteem and worthlessness. We have "the mind of Christ", as Paul tells us in 1 Corinthians 2:16. The Spirit of God is within us, so we have the capability and the gift of being able to know Christ. What a wonderful thing, that though He may be mysterious, we can have a sense of something more, something deeper, something holy. Something so much better than any idea of 'more' the world can throw at us. We are invited into a relationship with Jesus where we are able to mature and be healed because of what He reveals to us through His word and Spirit.

Meditate on His law, get to know the Word. Listen to podcasts, take your Bible *and* your notebook to church. Spend time each day in intimate communion with Jesus and learn His ways. Hear what He says about you, how He loves you and wants you to be whole and healed. When you struggle to move forward, choose to look to Jesus, the author and perfecter of your faith, walk with Him in suffering and ride with Him in glory.

Choose today to position yourself right before Jesus, just as you are; no editing, no photo shopping, no pretending. Just you, perfect you.

This, my friend, is the invitation, to more.

God is love. When we take up permanent residence in a life of love, we live in God and God lives in us. This way, love has the run of the house, becomes at home and mature in us, so that we're free of worry on Judgment Day—our standing in the world is identical with Christ's. There is no room in love for fear. Well-formed love banishes fear. Since fear is crippling, a fearful life—fear of death, fear of judgment—is one not yet fully formed in love.

---

1 JOHN: 4:17-18

The Message

Two
FATHER-LESS

I have been a Christian for decades. I became a Christian at the age of twelve and I am now in my forties. As a child and teenager, I went to summer camps and youth groups, studied the Bible, was baptised in the Holy Spirit, and exercised spiritual gifts. I was saved for sure and was going for God, yet as I grew older, I became more aware of my short comings and started to feel a crippling sense of dread.

Dread is defined as 'great fear' or 'apprehension'. I was gripped by a feeling that I wasn't good enough. I didn't believe I was really loved by God as much as everyone else and chiefly believed I was too broken to be used by God, ever. What I was experiencing was a counter-productive faith, by that I mean I believed all that God said was true, but I wasn't certain that it was actually true for me. In her book, *Anonymous*,

Alicia Britt Chole writes that "anchoring ourselves in God's word is close to impossible if in our hearts, we are unsure that God and His word are good." I was anchored without assurance that the anchor would really hold. I didn't know I was loved fully and completely.

Yet, knowing we are loved by our Father dispels our fear, our shame and our sense of worthlessness. We may have walked with God for years, which is wonderful, but it doesn't mean that we truly believe we are loved. This was precisely my experience.

Last spring, I attended an incredible women's conference, in Leeds. I was listening to the speaker, who was amazingly gifted at preaching. I honestly cannot remember what the main point of her message was, not because she wasn't brilliant, but because what arrested me was when all of a sudden, she said something like, "we are going to pray for the fatherless."

Well, great that's me. My father died when I was a little girl. This is *not* what I came for. Then two male speakers from the conference were invited onto the stage to pray for the fatherless. Well, all of heaven broke loose! It was messy, and it was wonderful. I cannot tell you what happened precisely, but I know that when I came to, after a holy and snotty moment, I was changed and it was glorious. I worshipped like I'd never worshipped before. I felt brave, I felt fearless and I *knew I was loved* by the Father.

I realise now how significant it was as God's spirit touched my spirit and confirmed who I really am. I am His child, I am no longer a slave to fear, I am His and He is mine. I felt accepted for the first time, by God in that moment. I knew then that I was adopted by my Heavenly Father. I *am* His and nothing can change that.

My father had died after a short illness when I was just six years old; my brother was four. We were left emotionally destitute. My mum had lost the love of her life and my brother and I had lost our security. I don't have many memories of my father as I was so young. I know he is gone but in so many ways I don't really know what I am missing. I don't know what his voice sounded like, what his aftershave smelt like, how his hand felt around mine, or the comfort of his lap. I do remember him teaching me to ride my bike in the back garden. I also remember the call from the hospital when he died. I remember when our hallway was lined with visitors after the funeral and their sympathetic smiles as they watched my brother and I walk past them. I remember having to move to a smaller house and feeling different because I didn't have a dad. We were always the family that was broken; we were never the same as everybody else. We were different, we still are. People were kind, don't get me wrong. They tried earnestly, with good intention not to let us feel that our family was different to theirs, but the reality was we would never be like them, ever.

Over the years as I grew in faith, I realise now that I had an unhealthy view of the Father's heart. I would avoid seminars and books about the subject because I didn't want to be pigeon-holed as 'the girl without a dad'. I didn't want to be boxed into the 'ah yes, she behaves that way because her dad died.' Experiencing bereavement is earth shattering. Of course, you are going to behave differently to those who've not gone through the same thing. I consciously avoided anything that would 'help' me because it all felt so inevitable and in truth, I felt patronised. I was hiding from God and although I hadn't abjectly sinned against Him, I was walking in nakedness, shame and the excruciating pain of loss.

Yet, in one moment at that conference I attended years later something shifted. God met me in a way that I've never known before. It trumps the first time I spoke in tongues, felt the Holy Spirit, prophesied, preached, you name it. This was THE moment that changed everything. Something in my spirit responded to the tender whisper of God's heart to my sense of depravation and emotional poverty.

My being fatherless had unwittingly become a bid to God to meet me with more of Himself, more of His Father's heart. My less became the perfect opportunity for God to be magnified and His glory revealed: for His grace to abound, for His love to be poured out and my heart to be filled to overflowing in His presence.

This is the call of God – that the title of the book you are holding suggests, that as we lean into our less, He calls us deeper into the more of His love. Sometimes plummeting the depths of love will be scary, but we will always find Love Himself there, waiting to catch us.

OUR LESS *IS* MORE SIMPLY BECAUSE THE VOID THAT OUR PAIN OF LESS CREATES, BECOMES THE MOST PERFECT CAVITY FOR MORE OF GOD.

My friend's dad died when she was just pre-school age. She says herself that the name 'Father' had so many painful and negative connotations to it, that for a long time she didn't know what a Good Father was. She lost her father in tragic circumstances and says that, *"Without a doubt God has turned anything that was intended for bad in my life to good. I was taught that God can do that, very early in life and it has been something I have clung to ever since."* This is a woman who has learned what it is to allow her pain of less to become that most perfect cavity for more of God.

Another dear friend's dad died when she was in adulthood but before she had her own children. When I asked her in what way God had proved He is more than enough, she said, *"Because nothing else will satisfy."* She holds firm to the truth that *"when we are faithless, He is faithful. He is enough because He is always there, He will never leave me nor forsake me."* Thank you, Lord. Again, another woman I am so proud of and who has allowed the void of grief to be filled to overflowing by the promise of God.

The less of being without *my* earthly father created the opportunity for God the Father to come in with all his goodness and love, with the spirit of adoption and bless me with *more*. The *more* of not just being loved, but adopted and not just a child, but a co-heir with Christ. This is the promise of more to the fatherless, to my friends, to all of us, should we choose to believe it.

And it's this spirit of adoption that God gives us that keeps us connected to Him. It's the spirit of God within us that allows us to cry "Daddy!" We can have that intimate relationship with Him. It is there for the taking and it absolutely does not bear any resemblance to your relationship with your earthly father. If your father is good, God is perfect, if your father is absent, He is a present help; if your father is critical, God is kind. You name it, God is *more*!

Recently some of our greatest friends adopted two amazing children. We have journeyed with them through the years of knowing they could not conceive, to considering IVF and then a few years of quiet until they both felt it was time to pursue parenthood via the avenue of adoption. My friend has been right in the thick of me having my babies and not once did I see her waiver with jealousy. She has gone beyond herself and carried her pain with such dignity and grace. She makes me beam, just thinking about her. She and her husband have been constant in our lives and journeyed with us through the last decade that we have become parents. Do not get me wrong, I love that I have had babies and am thankful that we've not had to face what our friends have had to, but you know what - I love their story more than mine. I love that adoption at its heart is totally and utterly redemptive. It is a story which has healing, rescue and restoration at the core of the narrative. I love their two children and all that they stand for. They are gorgeous, strong and courageous. They have been rescued from a dark place and promoted to a higher ground that offers hope, healing and love.

They will have much to face as they grow up, yet I know that as they own their story, they will become increasingly whole and even more free. I cannot wait to see what happens as the years unfold, as plenty of sweet times trump their pain with the biggest slam on the table. The crème de la crème of their story is that they are cherished children from the get-go. They were longed for from the start and so, my friend, are you.

In truth, I think that all too often we miss something truly remarkable about our very purpose and creation. We forget that we were longed for and created by love, in love, to love. We know that the enemy would have us believe we are no good, we are insignificant and useless, but that's simply not the case. The enemy wants us to believe that our brokenness ring fences our potential to the nth degree and that our fallen nature is beyond redemption.

Does knowing we are loved by the Father make a difference? Absolutely! Knowing we are loved by the Father means that we can live and breathe from a place of freedom, of security and of hope. Knowing we are loved makes a difference because we become fruitful. Insecurity, doubt, fear or shame will hold us back from going after the things that He has purposed for us. This seems to be the enemy's primary plan, to rob us of purpose. He will use the crippling emotions we experience to make us doubt our eternal use.

Again, Chole writes, "our emotions are not truth's vocal twin and feelings are not the litmus test for reality." Only God can be that line, that litmus paper and I think we should let Him be, since He is the creator of the universe!

Let's stop focusing so frequently on the reality of our fallen condition, rather than the potential of our Godly nature. Our fallen nature has left us not just disconnected but also dislocated and our journey of discovering our true origin seems to begin and end there. Yes, we are fallen, still we are not without hope. We know through Jesus there is redemption, but do you know your identity as being one embarrassed by shame and nakedness was never God's intention? Nor was its God's intention that our relationship with Him was broken. It is not God's ideal that you hide away and fear speaking to Him because of what you may or may not have done, or because of your pain. Hiding, fear and shame disconnect us from God and exacerbate that void more and more. The more shame we feel, the more fear we feel, the more fearful we feel the more we hide away.

Let's not forget though that in all of this, God the Father granted us the gift of freedom. What a glorious gift! However, it means that God doesn't coerce or cajole us into relationship or repentance. He has given us free will and a divine freedom which is born out of relationship with God and not a rejection of Him. Disconnection through disobedience, deception and devastation are the name of the enemy's game.

We need to do all we can to stand firm. We must and should lean into God more, to know Him more and feel even more known by Him if it were possible, so that each and every day we can walk in increasing and unrelenting freedom. If we allow ourselves to be convinced that we are unloved, useless and nothing, we will never step out wholeheartedly into the plans God has for us, because we don't believe for one second that we are worth it.

Karl Barth, in *The Humanity of God*, says that since God is the God of man, "it remains true that God who gave His Son to become and remain our brother assures us that He willed to love man, that He loved us and still loves us and shall love us because He chose and determined Himself to be our God."

He determined to be *our* God. He *chose* to be our God. He *chose* to be your God and mine and there's nothing you can do to change that fact.

Barth goes onto say that "man's God-given freedom is not to be sought and found in any solitary detachment from God. In God's own freedom there is encounter and communion; there is order and, consequently, dominion and subordination; there is majesty and humility, absolute authority and absolute obedience; there is offer and response."

TRUE FREEDOM CANNOT BE FOUND VOID OF GOD.

Misusing our God-given freedom is so painful. It leaves us desolate and destitute, lonely and without. It screams "you are broken and messed up." It says, "you are absolutely no good!" Yet our failing allows God to lift us up, hold us with hands of love and affirm us with words of grace. Our 'less' opens a door to an increased intimacy with God the Father should we choose to walk over the threshold.

Paul expresses so beautifully the truth of what Jesus'

coming and mission means for us, as we live in our fallen reality when he writes:

"He was supreme in the beginning and — leading the resurrection parade — He is supreme in the end. From beginning to end He's there, towering far above everything, everyone. So spacious is He, so roomy, that everything of God finds its proper place in Him without crowding. Not only that, but all the broken and dislocated pieces of the universe – people and things, animals and atoms – get properly fixed and fit together in vibrant harmonies, all because of His death, His blood that poured down from the cross. You yourselves are a case study of what He does. At one time you all had your backs turned to God, thinking rebellious thoughts of Him, giving Him trouble every chance you got. But now, by giving Himself completely at the Cross, actually dying for you, Christ brought you over to God's side and put your lives together, whole and holy in His presence" (Colossians 1:18-22, The Message).

This is the God; the perfect Father that we can know and love as He knows and loves us. The one who adopts us, who loves us fiercely, who lifts us up and who disciplines us, all for the purpose of developing character and Christlikeness deep within us. The one who beckons us to a deeper place of intimacy where we find healing and wholeness.

This is God; the model Father, who is *more* than your absent, abusive, angry Dad and connects His spirit to yours as you cry "Abba!" This is God; the perfect Father, who is *more* than your disappointments, your void of loss, your questions and confusion.

This is God; the faultless Father, who wants you, who chose you. He wants you to live fearlessly and freely. This is God; the perfect Father of *more*.

Therefore, since we are surrounded by so great a cloud of witnesses, let us also lay aside every weight and sin which clings so closely, and let us run with endurance the race that is set before us.

HEBREWS 12:1

English Standard Version

Three
TRUTH-LESS

In a bid to strengthen my fractured mental health, I had counselling to help me understand the change in my disposition. You know about the death of my father; a huge trigger indeed. A fall out with my best friend many years ago (we've since made up!) was another one. A bust up with our small group at church over a decision we made; another one. Not having our own home whilst pregnant with our daughter; another one. Leaving a church, we loved because we were called elsewhere; another one. A difficult time in our marriage that I was ready to walk out of the door; another. I felt rejected, unwanted, hated and insecure.

The feelings I was experiencing had taken residence in the very fibre of my being, meaning I was unable to live fully and abundantly as God intended. Whatever guise my pain was in I had inadvertently allowed myself to wear garb that wasn't intended for me. Instead of putting on the "new self", as described in Colossians 3:12-17, I had been subject to a rather less spiritual wardrobe. I was dressed in despair, covered in a cloud of critique and wearing the weight of sin and shame.

The lies I had believed shot straight into the essence of who I was. The *lies* became labels, and the *labels* gave way to entitlement or *licence*. I felt that life was unfair, I deserved better, it's their fault not mine, they owe me an apology. The lies I had believed clothed me from head to toe. I had exchanged a beautifully tailored garment of praise for off the peg rubbish, fast fashion. I soon realised I needed to take off the weight of what hindered me and urgently update my wardrobe.

Adam and Eve's story illustrates how easily this happened to me and to us all. The serpent's question posed to Eve in the Garden challenged her perception of what God had asked them to do and the boundaries He had set. Had Eve misunderstood the instructions from the Lord? Did God really say that? Aren't you made for more? You see it again, the cycle of lies, labels and licence.

Misconception is dangerous ground, because primarily it is inaccurate and if we're not careful, results in eternal damage to our tender souls. Slowly but surely, we become ensconced in attire that we weren't created for. Our nakedness and openness before God our Father become embarrassing and painful so we cover our true selves and our rightful identity, and we are left like toddlers denied what they want and screaming "that's not fair!"

So often we blame our pain for our broken sense of self. That's only the half of it. Often believing the lie is what started it all. Where do we need to acknowledge that we've been chatting with the enemy for too long? Pain isn't our enemy. Our conversation with the devil is. Dialoguing with the devil is dangerous.

Lysa TerKeurst, in her book, *Uninvited* writes, "Pain is not the enemy. Pain is the indicator that brokenness exists. Pain is the reminder that the real enemy is trying to take us out and bring us down by keeping us stuck in a broken place. Pain is the invitation for God to move in and replace our faltering strength with His." The lasting damage of our shame, control, fear and pain is the perfect atmosphere for our vulnerability to be used negatively against us, against our formation, maturity and identity.

PAIN HAS A CLEVER WAY OF STUNTING OUR SPIRITUAL GROWTH AND TURNING OUR HEARTS TO STONE.

We need to be reminded again that our true identity is that we are children of God, crafted by His hand and adorned in grace. We need to stop our lives giving way to a substandard false identity that is shaped by the deception spat at us by the father of lies. Unfortunately, this false identity takes president and becomes the central focus of our being and doing, yet it *is* completely false and so far removed from where God intends us to be. We allow our false sense of self to be nurtured. We settle for this, convinced that this is the best it's going to be. We believe that somehow life is now complete because we've filled our void of less with all the world's trappings and misguided sense of what constitutes an abundant life. Our false sense of self causes us to keep running from suffering, to self-medicate in numerous ways and live our lives comfortably in the hope that all the gains that we make, whether materially, financially or whatever, afford us eternal significance. Our souls become embroiled in lies, labels and licence; our view of God becomes distorted and the Father's roar of life in all its fullest is muted by doubt.

We see in Scripture that it only took one word, one moment, one pause of hesitation to change the course of human history - so why do we think we are immune? One word, one moment and we too, like Adam and Eve are left covered in fig leaves, full of shame and on the outside. As soon as Eve was on her own, the enemy moved straight in, sidled up to her and asked, 'Surely?" In one word the doubt is cast, and the questioning starts. In one moment, Eve's identity is challenged and her security unsettled. In one thought, Eve's false self is birthed and her true self squandered. Thus, mankind finds itself spending its entire lifetime maintaining, stroking and approving this false self, without realising that it's entirely self-centred and harmful to one's Kingdom influence. In Adam's Return, Richard Rohr notes that "the false self must be destabilised, or we will never know the true joy of being." In that moment in the Garden, Eve lost her 'joy of being' and instantly became a slave to doing.

Deception and entitlement are key tactics of the enemy and the leverage he needs to disable our thinking and paralyse any morsel of truth running through our veins. We live ruined, deceived and arrogant. The thing is, it takes only a moment for us to fall under his spell and regrettably a life time to break free from it. It's like hypnosis when we live bound by lies and deception because we do not actually realise that we are living in a false state of existence. It's no wonder then, that we have lost sense of whose we are and what we are called to do. Where do we need to toughen up, sharpen up, armour up? How do we break this cycle of lies, labels and licence?

We need to allow His Spirit to cut off all that throttles our chance of spiritual maturity. Lies have a clever way of inflaming a dormant bit of pain, subtly nestling closely into our vulnerability and slowly smothering it. We need to draw near again to Christ in repentance and allow Him to exchange our false sense of self for the true sense, which can only be found by surrendering to Christ. His roar of '*more*' to us as we wallow in false self is deafening. It's a cry of 'You are mine!' A sense of self, defined by Rohr as one "characterised by an inner abundance." This is the life we are called to, the life of truth, abundance and *more*.

That moment in the Garden has a lot to answer for. We know that we will spend from here until eternity batting Satan off our shoulders and walking in truth. Yet, it is helpful because it illustrates perfectly how unwittingly we can allow a lie to take a seat at our table. In the Garden we see how lies may look sweet to taste, how they fuel a blame culture and ultimately if we believe them long enough, they leave us exposed, vulnerable and distant from God. If you are in a cycle of blaming everyone else around you or feeling distant from God, ask yourself what are the lies you are believing right now, because you may be believing something that isn't in line with God's truth about you and your circumstance. Blaming your husband, your best mate or your sports coach, won't change it. You have to turn your attention back to God and His word and allow His Spirit to permeate every fibre of your being until you feel sure that you are functioning from a more whole place.

At the point at which doubt steps in, faith needs to rise and trample it out. The true self must be called forth, embraced fully and entirely surrendered to the Lordship of Christ, as Jesus reminds us: "If anyone would come after me, let him deny himself and take up his cross daily and follow me" (Luke 9:23).

Karl Martin writes in *Stand*, "Don't allow yourself to act in a way that is not consistent with the grace you have received in Jesus." He writes also that, "God invites us to so much more than we accept." So, it seems to me that to live a life that is freer and more whole, that is more truth-focused rather than shame-bound, we have to remind ourselves of this grace that we have received. It is the grace that covers over all our brokenness and mistakes. It is the power of the cross and the resurrection that means we do not have to live according to what we have been told we are, but rather according to *whose* we are. We are God's children, we are precious, we have purpose and destiny and we have a reason for existing. We are broken because of our poor choices, not because God is not being good.

For me to live in a place of shame insults what God has done in my life. To live inconsistently is to make a mockery of the fact that, in Him, we have fullness and a freedom that the world cannot match by a long way. We will have heard it said and read it written, that what the world offers is not a match for Kingdom living, but we still live like we are not convinced, don't we? Then quite rightly we should allow the Holy Spirit to convict us, help us move to saying sorry and re-direct our footsteps. We may stray, but the grace we have received is there to bring us back. We carry hope and potential; we have brilliant minds and incredible imaginations. I really believe that grace makes a way when nothing else seems possible. I see in my own life that grace has flung open doors to healed relationships, parenting and my marriage - writing this book even. I cannot do anything without the power and presence of God in my life. I want to accept even more of the grace that is on offer to me, I want to live more wholeheartedly, more fully and more honestly.

It's because of His grace that we are forgiven, and we are free. The only licence we have is that we are loved by God – and not because we deserve it or are entitled to it, but because He is good. He is love. Let the nature of who God is become your aspiration. Not things, not sex, not money, not power. Don't fight for control to be perfect or to have everything just as you like it. Live a life of self-sacrifice. Live a life led by Jesus. Let Him draw near enough to heal you and to exchange the lies you've so long believed, for truth. Let Him peel off the labels you are covered with and the clothes that don't suit you, so He can redress you in all that He intended for you.

YOU ARE NOT WHO YOU THINK YOU ARE; YOU ARE NOT WHO THEY SAY YOU ARE.

You are God's precious one and He loves you; fig leaves and all. This is the God who comes near and strips the weight of 'less' that you have lived under and clothes you in love. This is the God who loves you enough to redress you and redeem you. This is the God who beckons you to a life of surrender, that denies the 'less' the world offers and instead gives you the gift of *more* today and always.

Mary has chosen the good portion, which will not be taken away from her.

LUKE 10:42

English Standard Version

Four
GOD-LESS

We live in an age where we are swamped with activities, schedules, demands and noise. We struggle to fit 'time out' into our calendars, we long for a day when things will slow down, or for an extra hour to magically appear in any given 24-hour window. We are time poor; caught up in a whirlwind of over-scheduling and trying to make room for the people and the tasks that matter to us. To experience silence and solitude seems impossible to attain, least of all to carve out a few tender moments of communion with the Father.

One of the saving graces of my period of depression and anxiety was that I had to learn that time for me *and* time with God were both essential for my wellbeing. I had to learn to be kind to myself and try to master what Jesus meant when He encouraged the disciples to "learn the unforced rhythms of grace" (Matthew 11:29, The Message).

SELF-CARE ISN'T SELFISH, IT IS ESSENTIAL FOR OUR WELL-BEING, OUR MISSION AND OUR SERVICE.

John Ortberg notes and quotes Gordon MacDonald, in *Soul Keeping*, when he writes: "Our outer worlds are visible and measurable and expandable, they are easier to deal with. They demand our attention. *'The result is that our private world is often cheated, neglected because it does not shout quite so loudly.'*"

Ortberg and MacDonald are right. Life *is* loud. Demands and to-do lists scream for our attention. The urgency of 'doing' something drowns the necessity of 'being' when we seek to "be still and know God" (Psalm 46:10). I wonder how much time we spend getting ready for work in the morning, compared with the time we spend in prayer, or the fight to get the gym session squeezed in - ousting any hope of stopping to listen to what God is saying to us? Of course, we need both; self-care isn't just spiritual, it is physical, mental and emotional. Yet this is precisely why we need to make time for God, for both He and our spirituality is holistic.

LIFE ISN'T THE ENEMY OF OUR INTIMACY, OUR BUSYNESS IS.

Aaron Niequist in his book *The Eternal Current* writes, "Many of us live in a swirl of motion, and it's easy to let daily activities propel us forward without or ever dipping below the surface to notice what matters most."

Busyness banishes any chance of a bountiful time with the Lord and it robs us of perspective. If we are not careful, we push our intimate time with God to the periphery of our calendar, because the enemy has convinced us that it is of such little value anymore. The enemy will always wave attractive alternatives in front of us. There always seems to be a better offer and the grass always seems to be a little greener just over there. The enemy wants us to believe that somehow, we can live fully and free with God at arms-length and that time with God in any guise is an extravagance we cannot afford.

Bob Sorge, in *Secrets of the Secret Place*, observes that "Satan will employ whatever device will work – anything to keep you from being a person of one thing. The greatest dimensions of kingdom power will be touched by those who are truly ignited and energised by their personal love relationship with the Lord Jesus."

So, it is down to us to make good choices and instil sensible boundaries for, "I and no one else am responsible for the condition of my soul," as Ortberg reminds us in the aforementioned book, Soul Keeping. We need to decide if time with the Lord *is* food for the soul. We need to be intentional about keeping our souls conditioned and in union with the Lord. We need to adopt discipline with our scheduling and implement a structure that ensures in some way our time with Him is our greatest priority. We need to realise that time with the Lord has both daily and eternal benefit.

The late Dallas Willard described our souls well in

Renovation of the Heart, when he wrote: "Our soul is like a stream of water, which gives strength, direction and harmony to every other area of our life. When that stream is as it should be, we are constantly refreshed and exuberant in all we do, because our soul itself is then profusely rooted in the *vastness of God* and His kingdom, including nature; and all else within us is enlivened and directed by that stream."

Here we see again, the reality that we are in relationship with the God of more. Our soul, however small and 'less' it feels, joins with our great, creative and redemptive God whose sole charge is to capture our imagination and invite us into His story of salvation and redemption. He calls us to a life of self-denial and selflessness, if we are brave enough to exchange our 'less' for His abundant provision for our soul. Sorge writes too, that we absolutely "can't garner intimacy on the run. (We need) depth of connection." We need more than a five-minute prayer on the way to work, the two-minute arrow prayer on the school run, or the 30 second cry in the midst of chaos. These are good things of course, but our soul needs more than a moment to sustain itself, it needs constant and continual attention in the presence of God.

LIFE WITH CHRIST IS NOT FULL OF INTERMITTENT INSTALMENTS, IT IS A CURSIVE CONTINUUM.

So, in choosing to prioritise our time with God, the challenge we find before us is the fight for solace. We must push against the tidal wave of life and invite God into the depths of it. Our religiosity dictates that we must carve out a 'quiet time' - however life demands God at every turn, not just for five minutes when we wake. Yet, too we find that the discipline that this religiosity affords, is one that is rich with intimacy and steeped in the ability to truly change us.

Semantics has stolen the richness of a daily discipline and turned it into a practice that is seemingly dangerously legalistic. Instead, we need to remind ourselves that God's desire is to attend to our spiritual core. We need to become people of rhythm rather than balance, finding God all day, every day. We need also to shift our thinking about our devotional time with God from being a religious duty to becoming a deep and strengthening joy. Our time with God is our life blood, not a job to be done.

Our minds are prone to wondering. We know that there are too many distractions: social media, one more load of laundry, another errand, a phone call, an urgent meeting, a bit of DIY. It is important that we do fight for our intimacy with Jesus, for the sake of the world and for the sake of our hearts. We need to be deliberate – choose the tough call, set the alarm, interrupt our plans and just be good old fashioned disciplined. To tick the 'quiet time' off the to do list each day isn't for the purpose of segregating our lives, but rather to enrich, empower and give purpose to the remainder of our day. For the fullness that Jesus speaks of in John 10:10 is not a life that is a frenzy of over-scheduling but an abundant and fruitful one, bearing witness to the Lord of time and the holder of our destiny.

The blessed irony is that our lives which are intended to be lived fully and intimately with Christ, often leave us running at a deficit. We rummage around living in a sorrowful state of 'less', instead of living in all that the God of 'more' has promised. Yet in this very contemporary struggle with time and agenda, we *do* find God. In our overwhelmed state, we can meet with the One who calms the storm and stills our hearts if we dare to stop and savour the beauty of His presence.

To submit yourself to the daily practice of Examen, an ancient practice of prayer and confession for example, might seem to some a little legalistic, but it's laced with invitation to find more of God. Indeed, it echoes something of John the Baptist's cry in John 3:30, "He must increase, I must decrease" as you allow God to search your heart, hear your confession and restore your soul.

Ancient practice is old, but it's not outdated. It has stood the test of time because *our hearts have stood its testing* and we are better people for having time with God that is set aside intentionally and wholeheartedly.

Jesus extended a beautiful invitation to us when He said: "Live in me. Make your home in me just as I do in you. In the same way that a branch can't bear grapes by itself but only by being joined to the vine, you can't bear fruit unless you are joined with me" (John 15: 4-8, The Message).

Jesus bids us to move in with Him and to be intimate with Him. Don't just know about Him, but dwell in Him, take refuge in Him and make a shelter in Him. All relationships take time, work and commitment. They require investment and self-sacrifice, but this commitment is best expressed in staying connected, keeping close and aligning ourselves with Christ.

I wonder what knowing the impact of our determination to steal ourselves away for just a moment would have? I wonder if we understand the implications of what it means to set apart time to be *silent* with our Saviour. It seems that we possess, as Earling Kagge discerns in his book, *Silence*, "a fear of getting to know ourselves better." If we spend time with the Lord, what's the worst that could happen? He convicts us of sin. He disciplines us. He tells us that

He loves us. He lets us know that we don't have to worry or be afraid. Time out with the Father is necessary for the transformation of our souls and the broadening of our perspectives. If Jesus took time out with His Father, we would be unwise not to. To be still before God, with only the silence listening - what an incredible way to start a day, before children or chores or work or commuting start vying for our attention. As we become quieter on the inside, we connect with God in a deeper way. In the silence there is no 'great divide' or 'veil', no words to hide behind, just us and our hearts laid bare before God. When we allow earthy distractions to be muted by holy silence, we hear afresh God's heart of love and longing and our souls are restored.

In the quiet, we journey to the secret place of transformation and change. In the stillness, we draw near to God and He draws near to us. In the inactivity and the solitude, we discover more of who we are meant to be. In the hush, the presence of God overwhelms us, and we are forever changed by His gift of abundance, His offering of more - more life, more peace, more time, more perspective, more power, more effectiveness, more salt and more light.

In setting aside time to commune with God, to really meet with Him in a meaningful way, we are blessed beyond belief. God is longing to meet with us, to talk with us, to encourage us, to affirm us and for us to hear Him "singing over us" (Zephaniah 3:17). The joy is that the gift of God Himself is found in the stillness. He is the one who leads us "beside still waters" (Psalm 23:2) and in His presence, we find peace. Being with Him is worth every rearranged diary, every good intention and every second of silence. When we choose to lay aside our agenda and our diaries, to shut the door and dampen the sound of the world around us, we find God and His glorious gift of more, again.

It's in Christ that we find out who we are and what we are living for. Long before we first heard of Christ and got our hopes up, He had his eye on us, had designs on us for glorious living, part of the overall purpose He is working out in everything and everyone.

EPHESIANS 1:11-12

The Message

Five
PURPOSE-LESS

Purpose, calling, vocation – whatever you wish to call it, we are born with it and we live *and* strive to fulfil it. It is a peculiar paradox of our faith and relationship with God - yes, *in* Him we find out what we are living for (Ephesians 1:1), and too, we have purpose and significance because we have been formed *by* Him (Isaiah 43:7). Yet somehow, even if we can grasp this – honestly at times we rarely live in the fullness of what it means. Essentially, we are here very much because it was our Creator's intention and each and every one of us was made for an assignment with eternal significance. I know that I have forfeited many years wondering why I am here and what I am living for. I have wasted time making my purpose the object of my pursuit, rather than pursuing the One who ordains everything that I am here to do. Feeling purpose-less is the perfect catalyst for depression and comparison to take hold.

We are all created with purpose. We know that because we are formed by God Himself - yet so easily we let insecurity become our voice of reason as we struggle to find purpose in why we are here and what it is all for. Insecurity, coupled with an addiction to comparison, means our fruitfulness lacks and our growth is stemmed.

Some of my contemporaries are pastors of influential churches, leading worship all over the world and speaking at major conferences – and then there is little old me. I lead worship, preach, help on the kids team and write when I am able to. Both ends of this spectrum of ministry demand faithfulness, irrespective of where you might fall on this curve of experience and opportunity. So often I have fallen into the trap of believing that what I am doing isn't significant because it isn't publicly recognised, rather than celebrating my faithful contribution to a global church, working in unity to usher in the Kingdom of God. At times, I know I have dismissed my effectiveness and contribution in my local church, simply because I am not on the world stage! This attitude has distracted me and exacerbated that insecurity that I previously mentioned. Just because I don't have a platform does not mean my contribution to the Kingdom of God isn't valid or without impact; nor do I need a platform or a world stage to validate anything I do unto Him.

YOUR LOCAL CHURCH NEEDS YOU TO BE PLANTED, COMMITTED AND FAITHFUL.

Purpose isn't about worldly or even Christian validation, although a little encouragement goes a long way! It is about realising that we can and do contribute to a far bigger and greater eternal picture. We are part of something significant that will change the face of the earth, meaning people will bow down and worship as more and more accept Christ's invitation to follow Him and become 'fishers of men' (Matthew 4:19).

As a Christian, if I believe my primary purpose is to write a book for the sake of writing a book, then it serves no purpose. If, however, the chief aim of writing a book is to draw readers closer to Jesus and encourage them towards a more lasting Christlikeness, then it's served its purpose. If I teach for the sake of teaching, then there's no lasting impact. If I believe I can impact the children I teach with any virtue I possess akin to Christ, then I am making strides towards finding eternal purpose in my every day. The list goes on: engineering, parenting, financial services and cleaning. Am I making the most of every opportunity to "go therefore and make disciples of all nations, baptising them in the name of the Father and of the Son and of the Holy Spirit" (Matthew 28:19), and ultimately fulfilling the most significant purpose of all?

TO GO AND MAKE DISCIPLES, IS WHY WE ARE SAVED AND THE VISION WE SERVE.

We must stop living our lives, asking the wrong questions. It is imperative that we stop asking, "What am *I* doing with my life?" and instead ask, "What is *God* doing *through* my life?" This is the place, the time, the position that I find myself in, where I am called to faithfully serve Him. I don't need to be perfect or whole – all that is required of me is to serve

Him with a sincere heart. Today, my season is as a mother of school-aged children, prior to this, I was working in the world of Visual Merchandising and for a schools work charity. Each one of these roles has mattered and does matter to God, because they have set me right in the centre of a broken and hurting world.

There is purpose where God has positioned us – we might not always feel like this is the case, or even believe it, but we need to remember that we aren't just saved for our own sake, but for the sake of the world also. Look at the example of Christ – everything He did was for something far bigger and greater than that moment. Yes, every miracle was a miracle indeed for it had purpose to heal, save and redeem, yet it also contributed to the glorious and magnificent eternal purpose of why Jesus came – He came to seek and to save the lost (Luke 19:10).

There is no better place to be, however the enemy would try to convince us otherwise. As I've mentioned before, he tries to let us believe that we are unable to contribute anything worthwhile. So, we need to come back to the truth of God's word that says we are formed *with* a purpose and we are saved *for* a purpose.

Self-doubt has a cruel way of making us butt heads with our potential, rather than embrace it. It stands in the way of our destiny and God's divine intention for our lives. All the while we settle for this state of mediocrity, our momentum is hindered. Self-doubt is another cruel tactic of the enemy, to disable our destiny and prevent our purpose. So, when it kicks in, perhaps we should read books, such as this one, packed with promise that we will live more fully, wholeheartedly and purposefully. Or listen to podcasts, attend a conference and go on a retreat. All are hugely effective, but good as they are, they will only sustain us for *so* long. What we need is to reset ourselves! We need to come back to God. We need to take time to remember that any fulfilment of anything worthwhile is not and will never be down to us and our 'wholeness' – it will always be empowered by God – as we adopt a posture of humility and weakness. When we come to God in our feeling of being unable and being less than we hoped, He faithfully meets us, strengthens us by His power and uses us for His glory. He draws near to us and by His Spirit, renews us with our sense of purpose, of knowing who we are and what our lives are for.

We know that we come from God, fashioned and formed by His hand. Our creation and formation *are* bespoke. We are each individually crafted for a unique purpose. We can make a unique contribution to the redemption of our world. We can be part of this amazing plan of restoration that God is longing to see happen through the saving of souls and the care of creation. Our origin was considered and inspired by God. We read in Genesis 1:26 that together with the Son and the Spirit, the Father created us in His own image. God is the creative designer that trumps all others. Talented couture designers do not have the same creative innovation that God does. Couture they may be, but divine they are not.

The psalmist writes, "For You formed my inward parts; You knitted me together in my mother's womb" (Psalm 139:13). I am certain that the use of the word 'knit' isn't an accident. It speaks brilliantly of our fashioning. Loop by loop, stitch by stitch, we were knitted together in our mother's womb. When you knit, you follow a pattern to make a garment that is fit for purpose and responsive to motion. We were knitted together in order that we would be responsive; able to stretch and be elastic for the one who determines our function and purpose. We aren't a tough old bit of leather or a robust upholstery fabric, we are knitted – allowing us to stretch and adapt to whatever direction God takes us. Our shape and our pattern have been considered and designed, and here we are today as a fulfilment of God's labour of love and commitment to His creative project.

WE ARE SPECIFICALLY DESIGNED, AT A SUITABLE STANDARD, SO WE ARE ABLE TO SUBMIT TO GOD'S SHIFTING AND STIRRING.

Our origin isn't an accident. It was intentional. Whether we were wanted or not, God wanted us. Whether we are the product of a one-night stand, a rape, or a loving relationship, God wanted us and intended us to be here. We are not products of our circumstances; we were handmade and handpicked by the Lord and to be part of His story, right here, right now. Just as with Adam and Eve, who were unashamedly naked in the garden (Genesis 2:25), God intended us to live in the same freedom. Adam and Eve were able to walk with God because of their lack of shame and insecurity about their nakedness. It is this same sense of freedom and being laid bare which enables us to have this connectedness with God. It is disastrous that the enemy cripples us constantly in many different ways, to deter us from living gloriously.

We are fashioned by God for purpose and He uses many things such as our origin, our culture and our destiny to form us, yet we know all too well that there is no quick fix for being transformed. Whilst our origin and other things are indeed formational, they don't always afford us results in the timeframe that we might like. We are naturally impetuous and impatient, looking for the next 'fix' and chucking out the things that do not seem relevant anymore. We are slow to yield to God's tender hand that gently takes away the parts of us that do not look like Him. Are we not urged by Paul to keep "our eyes fixed on Jesus" (Hebrews 12:2) and to remember the promise and potential contained within us (Ephesians 2:10)? Jesus longs for us to fulfil our potential and to bear fruit (John 15:2), so He lovingly tends and prunes us. His promise is that He will do "far more abundantly than all we ask or think" (Ephesians 3:20). Often, we are distracted from keeping our eyes on Him, as we keep looking over our shoulder, wondering if any earthly distraction will dare to attempt to prove its worth in the face of such holiness.

> **CHRISTLIKENESS CAN'T BE AIRDROPPED. HOLINESS IS NOT AVAILABLE ON PRIME. FORMATION TAKES TIME.**

We don't want to be robbed for a moment longer. We don't want to be "tossed by the wind" (James 1:6), in a wave of indecision that means we don't live for God, or anything else either. We certainly need to ask

God for wisdom as the word says. When we find ourselves without purpose, we become unproductive in the Kingdom of God. We spiritually flatline, our zeal is quenched and our sense of direction is lost.

We need to embrace the truth of who we're made by, fashioned by and created by – so we can live free and live with purpose. We need to lift our gaze and remind ourselves that our goal is bigger than happiness and comfort and that we must aim for more than what world recognition or stage presence offers us. The goal is indeed heaven, the purpose is to gather more followers of Christ and the glory is God's alone.

To those who have spent many years in the wilderness of uncertainty, hear the whisper of God's heart that calls you out onto the water. The bid to come and walk with Him. Your life was never meant to be mediocre; it was and is meant to be lived in steps of faith on the water. You are "the light of the world" (Matthew 5:14), so know that you should not be hidden, you were born to be on show - not on stage, but on display to a world that needs Jesus, so that every soul might hear the invitation from the God of *more* to follow Him, to walk with Him, to spend eternity with Him.

So, I invite you to start to tell your story, bring your offering and see what God will do as you engage with the world around you. Wait and see the miracle that the God of 'more' will do with the life of 'less' you bring Him.

CLOSING WORDS

I don't know where you find yourself as you close the pages of this book. I hope you have drawn closer to the One who has made you and is your champion. I pray that the Lord has stirred your heart to believe that you are able to do more than you can imagine – as you serve Him who is able to do immeasurably more than you can *ever* imagine. I hope you are yearning for more of Him - for more of His presence as you continue to trust Him and believe that He will meet you because of the 'less' that you hold in your hands.

I was reminded again of the power of 'less', as I re-read the story of the widow who had a small jar of olive oil, and the boy who had a humble packed lunch - both offered what they had.

GOD GRATEFULLY RECEIVED THE 'LESS' THAT THEY HAD.

He considered their offering enough to perform a miracle through. He wasn't dismissive, nor was He ungrateful. He received it gladly because He saw the potential in what she offered from her kitchen and what he offered from his hands. He thinks the same about you – and the little you bring. He *receives* it. Your 'less' is acceptable to Him - He sees the potential and wants to turn it into something beautiful, multiple and more.

Today is the day to stop living like you're depleted and not enough. Today is the day to start walking in the truth that God sees potential for miracle after miracle, in and through your life.

Together, let's start walking in this truth and see what a difference our 'less' can really make in the Kingdom of our God of 'more'.

To all who have been involved in this project,
thank you for cheering me on.

Bibliography

Karl Barth, The Humanity of God, HarperCollins Distribution Services (Oct. 1967)

Alicia Britt Chole, Anonymous, Thomas Nelson (1 Sept. 2011)

Brené Brown, The Gifts of Imperfection, Hazelden FIRM; 1st Edition (11 Jan. 2018)

Earling Kagge, Silence, Penguin (4 Oct. 2018)

Karl Martin, Stand, Muddy Pearl; UK ed. edition (22 Nov. 2013)

Aaron Niequist, The Eternal Current, Waterbrook Press (A Division of Random House Inc) (7 Aug. 2018)

John Ortberg, Soul Keeping, Zondervan; Special edition (6 May 2014)

Richard Rohr, Adam's Return, Independent Publishers Group (1 Oct. 2004)

Bob Sorge, Secrets of the Secret Place, Van Schaik Publishers (1 Jan. 2000)

Lysa TerKeurst, Uninvited, Thomas Nelson (22 Sept. 2016)

Simon P Walker, The Undefended Leader, Piquant Editions (9 May 2010)

Dallas Willard, Renovation of the Heart, IVP; U.K. ed edition (15 Nov. 2002)

ABOUT LOU

Lou Shorey is a coffee drinking writer, runner, beach lover and bookworm. She is married to Simon, a curate for the Church of England. They live in West Sussex with their four children.

Less is More is her first book.

@LouShorey